For

For Helen, Valerie, and Alex

Copyright © 1989
Peter Pauper Press, Inc.
202 Mamaroneck Avenue
White Plains, NY 10601
All Rights Reserved
ISBN 0-88088-256-5
Library of Congress No. 89-60649
Printed in Hong Kong
7   6   5

Contents

Golf and Tennis

If you are caught on a golf course during a storm and are afraid of lightning, hold up a 1-iron. Not even God can hit a 1-iron.

LEE TREVINO

Golfer's prayer: May I live long enough to shoot my age.

Playing golf is not hot work. Cutting sugar cane for a dollar a day is hot work.

CHI CHI RODRIGUEZ

The income tax has made liars out of more Americans than golf.

WILL ROGERS

We all choke. You're not human if you haven't. We get just as nervous as the average guy playing for the club championship.

CURTIS STRANGE

The major championships always come down to the last nine holes. . . . It takes character to win a major championship.

NICK PRICE

The ground shakes when she (JoAnne Carner) drives a ball.

SANDRA PALMER

Ben (Hogan) was tough. But I enjoyed playing with him. He never said anything and let me concentrate on my game.

SAM SNEAD

There's no such thing as natural touch. Touch is something you create by hitting millions of golf balls.

LEE TREVINO

Money was never a goal for me because of my amateur training. I was taught to win, and that was it.

JOANNE CARNER

If a lot of people gripped a knife and fork like they do a golf club, they'd starve to death.

SAM SNEAD

She (Judy Rankin) is so small, she might get lost in an unreplaced divot.

BOB TOSKI

You all know Jerry Ford—the most
dangerous driver since Ben Hur.

BOB HOPE

Well, how do you like my game?
I suppose it's all right, but I still prefer golf.

MILDRED MEIERS
and JACK KNAPP

A decision of the courts decided that the
game of golf may be played on Sunday, not
being a game within the view of the law,
but being a form of moral effort.

STEPHEN LEACOCK

I'm the best. I just haven't played yet.

MUHAMMAD ALI,
when asked about his golf game

Golf and sex are about the only things you can enjoy without being good at.

JIMMY DEMARET

Sam (Snead) doesn't know a dam' thing about the golf swing. But he does it better than anyone else.

BEN HOGAN

A golf course is the epitome of all that is purely transitory in the universe, a space not to dwell in, but to get over as quickly as possible.

JEAN GIRAUDOUX

Golf: a game in which you claim the privileges of age, and retain the playthings of childhood.

SAMUEL JOHNSON

Years ago we discovered the exact point, the dead center of middle age. It occurs when you are too young to take up golf and too old to rush up to the net.

FRANKLIN P. ADAMS

I regard golf as an expensive way of playing marbles.

G. K. CHESTERTON

The golf links lie so near the mill
   That almost every day
The laboring children can look out
   And see the men at play.

SARAH N. CLEGHORN (1915)

It is impossible to imagine Goethe or Beethoven being good at billiards or golf.

H. L. MENCKEN

I don't say my golf game is bad, but if I grew tomatoes, they'd come up sliced.

MILLER BARBER

Playing in the U. S. Open is like tippy-toeing through hell.

JERRY MCGEE

Golf is the most fun you can have without taking your clothes off.

CHI CHI RODRIGUEZ

I do much of my creative thinking while golfing. If people know you are working at home they think nothing of walking in for a cup of coffee. But they wouldn't dream of interrupting you on the golf course.

HARPER LEE,
author

A sick appendix is not as difficult to deal with as a five-foot putt.

GENE SARAZEN

Golf is a good walk spoiled.

MARK TWAIN

A lot more people beat me now.

DWIGHT D. EISENHOWER,
*explaining what happened to his golf game
after leaving the White House*

One of the advantages bowling has over golf is that you seldom lose a bowling ball.

DON CARTER,
bowling great

Golf is a game whose aim is to hit a very small ball into an even smaller hole, with weapons singularly ill-designed for the purpose.

WINSTON CHURCHILL

Golf seems to me an arduous way to go for a walk. I prefer to take the dogs out.

PRINCESS ANNE

If you watch a game, it's fun. If you play it, it's recreation. If you work at it, it's golf.

BOB HOPE

Tennis adds years to your life and life to your years.

ROY WILDER

Being champion is all well and good, but you can't eat a crown.

ALTHEA GIBSON DARBON,
on her retirement from tennis

Tennis is a perfect combination of violent action taking place in an atmosphere of total tranquility.

BILLIE JEAN KING

I think self-awareness is probably the most important thing towards being a champion.

BILLIE JEAN KING

The problem is that when you get [experience], you're too damned old to do anything about it.

JIMMY CONNORS

I hate to lose more than I like to win. I hate to see the happiness on their faces when they beat me.

JIMMY CONNORS

Everybody loves success, but they hate successful people.

JOHN MCENROE

It is vital, in my opinion, that tennis maintains a strong and watchful stand against swearing.

JOHN MCENROE,
infamous for his poor sportsmanship

Winners aren't popular. Losers often are.

VIRGINIA WADE
English tennis star

Football

Football players, like prostitutes, are in the business of ruining their bodies for the pleasure of strangers.

MERLE KESSLER

I love football. I really love football. As far as I'm concerned, it's the second best thing in the world.

JOE NAMATH

I can say with a clear conscience that I have never knowingly bit another football player. For one thing, I believe in good hygiene.

CONRAD DOBLER,
*in response to charges that
he had bitten a rival player*

Coach, some day when the going gets
rough, tell the boys to win one for the
Gipper.

GEORGE GIPP,
on his deathbed, to Knute Rockne

I had pro offers from the Detroit Lions and
Green Bay Packers, who were pretty hard
up for linemen in those days. If I had gone
into professional football the name Jerry
Ford might have been a household word
today.

GERALD FORD,
when serving as Vice President

We're basically a save-the-whales team; we
can't turn down big people who can play.

GEORGE YOUNG,
N.Y. Giants general manager

Pro football is like nuclear warfare. There
are no winners, only survivors.

FRANK GIFFORD

Is it normal to wake up in the morning in a sweat because you can't wait to beat another human's guts out?

JOE KAPP.
Minnesota Vikings quarterback

You have to decide if the experience you will have is worth the pain you will feel.

JACK YOUNGBLOOD.
L. A. Rams defensive end

If you can't explain it, how can you take credit for it?

HAROLD "RED" GRANGE
Chicago Bears halfback, on his talent for eluding tacklers

Rugby is a beastly game played by gentlemen; soccer is a gentleman's game played by beasts; football is a beastly game played by beasts.

HENRY BLAHA

Football is a game designed to keep coal miners off the streets.

JIMMY BRESLIN

In life as in a football game, the principle to follow is: Hit the line hard.

THEODORE ROOSEVELT

Sport is a product of human culture. America seems to need football at this stage of our social development. When you get ninety million people watching a single game on television, it . . . shows you that people need something to identify with.

JOE PATERNO,
Penn State coach

If you've never been tackled by L.T. (Lawrence Taylor), don't feel bad about it. Believe me, there are better things you can do with your time.

ERIC DICKERSON

If their IQs were five points lower, they would be geraniums.

RUSS FRANCIS,
on defensive linemen

I do believe that my best hits border on felonious assault.

JACK TATUM

You go for it. All the stops are out. Caution is to the wind, and you're battling with everything you have. That's the real fun of the game.

DAN DIERDORF,
St. Louis Cardinals offensive tackle

Some people try to find things in this game or put things into it which don't exist. Football is two things. It's blocking and tackling.

ANONYMOUS

I've never known of a football writer who ever had to stand up to a blitz.

JOE NAMATH,
N. Y. Jets quarterback

The man who complains about the way the ball bounces is likely the one who dropped it.

LOU HOLTZ,
U. of Arkansas football coach

My definition of a good runner is that he's *insane*—he does wild things, stuff you never see, and he does it spontaneously. Even he doesn't know what he's going to do next.

O. J. SIMPSON,
running back

When everything else breaks down, I don't hesitate to roam out of the pocket and do the boogaloo.

FRAN TARKENTON,
*N. Y. Giants and Minnesota
Vikings quarterback*

When I'm running well, my mind just goes blank. I'm not thinking about anything at all. Thinking is what gets you caught from behind.

O. J. SIMPSON

A school without football is in danger of deteriorating into a medieval study hall.

VINCE LOMBARDI

Embarrassment is a great motivator. There are some people who play very, very well just so they don't get embarrassed in front of their friends and a national audience.

LYNN SWANN
Pittsburgh Steelers wide receiver

When it comes to football, God is prejudiced—toward big, fast kids.

CHUCK MILLS

Coaches and Managers

Going to bed with a woman never hurt a
ball player. It's staying up all night looking
for them that does you in.

CASEY STENGEL

There are only two kinds of coaches—those
who have been fired and those who will be
fired.

KEN LOEFFLER,
basketball coach

I ought to retire right now. Steve Fisher is
unbeaten, untied and the happiest man
alive.

STEVE FISHER,
*after going 6-0 to win NCAA's as
"interim" coach of Michigan basketball*

Baseball is almost the only orderly thing in a very unorderly world. If you get three strikes, even the best lawyer in the world can't get you off.

BILL VEECK,
Chicago White Sox owner

Before the season, we took a survey of the fans and found out they want to see home runs more than anything else. So we went out to build a pitching staff to oblige them.

CLARK GRIFFITH,
Minnesota Twins

Good pitching will always stop good hitting, and vice versa.

CASEY STENGEL

A coach likes to have a lot of those old trained pigs who'll grin and jump right in the slop for him.

DARRELL ROYAL,
U. of Texas football coach

I had no trouble communicating. The players just didn't like what I had to say.

FRANK ROBINSON
Cleveland Indians manager

Nobody is hurt. Hurt is in the mind. If you can walk, you can run.

VINCE LOMBARDI

Whenever I decided to release a guy, I always had his room searched first for a gun. You couldn't take chances with some of those birds.

CASEY STENGEL

When you're playing for the national championship, it's not a matter of life or death. It's more important than that.

DUFFY DAUGHERTY,
Michigan State football coach

Listen, if you start worrying about the people in the stands, before too long you're up in the stands with them.

TOM LASORDA
L. A. Dodgers manager

Cut me and I'll bleed Dodger blue.

TOM LASORDA

Nobody had to tell Richard Burton he was a great actor. Nobody has to tell Frank Sinatra he is a great singer. Nobody has to tell Robert Wagner he's handsome. Nobody has to tell me I'm a good manager.

TOM LASORDA

If one of them jumps out of the stands like the other night, I'd punch him out in a Minnesota second.

BILLY MARTIN,
N. Y. Yankees manager,
about Yankee Stadium fans

It's a lot tougher to be a football coach than a President. You've got four years as President, and they guard you. A coach doesn't have anyone to protect him when things go wrong.

HARRY S TRUMAN

A manager's job is simple. For 162 games you try not to screw up all that smart stuff your organization did last December.

EARL WEAVER

I probably couldn't play for me. I wouldn't like my attitude.

JOHN THOMPSON,
Georgetown basketball coach

Defeat is worse than death, because you have to live with defeat.

BILL MUSSELMAN,
basketball coach

I was in the game for love. After all, where else can an old-timer like me with one leg, who can't hear or see, live like a king while doing the only thing I wanted to do?

BILL VEECK.

A team should be an extension of the coach's personality. My teams were arrogant and obnoxious.

AL MCGUIRE
former basketball coach

When we have a good team at Alabama, I know it's because we have boys who come from good Mamas and Papas.

BEAR BRYANT.
Alabama football coach

The way things are going for me, if I'd buy a pumpkin farm, they'd cancel Halloween.

BILLY GARDNER.
Minnesota Twins manager

I give the same halftime speech over and over. It works best when my players are better than the other coach's players.

CHUCK MILLS,
Wake Forest football coach

It isn't the size of the dog in the fight, but the size of the fight in the dog that counts.

WOODY HAYES,
Ohio State U. football coach

The two of them deserve each other. One's a born liar, the other's convicted.

BILLY MARTIN,
N. Y. Yankee manager, referring to
Yankee star Reggie Jackson
and owner George Steinbrenner

In order to keep doing what we've done, we have to keep doing what we've done in the past.

EARL WEAVER

Nice guys finish last.

LEO DUROCHER,
*on replacing the gentlemanly
but none-too-successful Mel Ott
as N. Y. Giants manager*

I've checked my heart. I don't have one.

JOHN MCKAY,
U. S. C. Trojans coach

Whew, I thought we would have to call in
the fire department, my team's so hot.

CASEY STENGEL,
*after his N. Y. Mets
ended a 17-game losing streak*

You can be smart and be a dumb player or
be dumb and be a smart player, but the
player or manager who does best is one
with good baseball judgment.

EARL WEAVER

It was like a heart transplant. We tried to implant college in him but his head rejected it.

BARRY SWITZER,
*U. of Oklahoma football coach,
on player who dropped out of school*

If you aren't fired with enthusiasm, you will be fired with enthusiasm.

VINCE LOMBARDI

Managing is getting paid for home runs someone else hits.

CASEY STENGEL,
on the art of managing

Not bad. Most people my age are dead. You could look it up.

CASEY STENGEL,
asked how he was doing

Winning isn't everything, but wanting to win is.

VINCE LOMBARDI

Show me a good loser and I'll show you a loser.

UNKNOWN

Show me a good loser and I'll show you an idiot.

LEO DUROCHER

No coach ever won a game by what he knows; it's what his players have learned.

BEAR BRYANT

That first year of retirement was a year of mourning, a year of reflection and grieving. You see, I'd spent my whole life with the game as my main force, and when it was gone, there was a terrible, aching hollow within me.

PAT RILEY,
L. A. Lakers coach

Sweat plus sacrifice equals success.

CHARLES O. FINLEY
Oakland Athletics owner

As men get older, the toys get more expensive.

MARVIN DAVIS,
Oakland Athletics owner, on
purchase of a professional team

You don't save a pitcher for tomorrow. Tomorrow it may rain.

LEO DUROCHER

I never got many questions about my managing. I tried to get 25 guys who didn't ask questions.

EARL WEAVER

It's what you learn after you know it all that counts.

EARL WEAVER,
Baltimore Orioles Manager

Basketball and Boxing

Me missing three free throws is like Vanna
White turning over the wrong letter.

MIKE GMINSKI,
N. J. Nets center

Any American boy can be a basketball star
if he grows up, up, up.

BILL VAUGHAN

The game is my wife. It demands loyalty
and responsibility, and it gives me back
fulfillment and peace.

MICHAEL JORDAN,
Chicago Bulls basketball star

Basketball games are the only place you
can yell at millionaires.

LEON THE BARBER

The man doesn't live on Earth. He just shows up on Earth for practice and game days.

BOB JEFFELATO,
describing Michael Jordan

The sun doesn't shine in the gym.

KIKI VANDEWEGHE,
on why he never had a tan in Los Angeles

It's really great being Magic Johnson the basketball player for eight months and then just plain Earvin Johnson for the other three.

MAGIC JOHNSON,
L. A. Lakers guard

Even if I'd known why he couldn't shoot foul shots, I'd never have told him.

BILL RUSSELL,
discussing his arch-rival, Wilt Chamberlain

Superman don't need no seat belt.

MUHAMMAD ALI,
when a stewardess asked him
to fasten his seat belt

Superman don't need no airplane, either.

STEWARDESS,
whereupon Ali fastened his belt

Honey, I forgot to duck.

JACK DEMPSEY,
to his wife, after losing to Gene Tunney

The possession of muscular strength and the courage to use it in contests with other men for physical supremacy does not necessarily imply a lack of appreciation for the finer and better things of life.... A man's vocation is no measure for the inner feelings nor a guarantee of his earnest desire to live right and attain the highest standards.

JACK JOHNSON,
first black heavyweight
champion of the world

The bigger they come the harder they fall.

BOB FITZSIMMONS

You can map out a fight plan or a life plan, but when the action starts, it may not go the way you planned, and you're down to your reflexes—which means your training. That's where your roadwork shows. If you cheated on that in the dark of the mornin', well, you're gettin' found out now under the bright lights.

JOE FRAZIER

I am not an animal in my personal life. But in the ring there is an animal inside me. Sometimes it roars when the first bell rings. Sometimes it springs out later in a fight. But I can always feel it there, driving me and pushing me forward. It is what makes me win. It makes me enjoy fighting.

ROBERTO DURAN

Float like a butterfly, sting like a bee.

Ali's boxing credo,
devised by aide Drew "Bundini" Brown

I'll be so fast that he'll think he's surrounded. I'm going to hit him before God gets the news.

MUHAMMAD ALI,
before title fight with George Foreman

My toughest fight was with my first wife.

MUHAMMAD ALI.

I just said I'm the greatest. I never said I was the smartest.

CASSIUS CLAY,
[later, MUHAMMAD ALI],
when rejected for military service

My heart says yes but my brain says no. I feel fortunate to get out of the ring with my faculties and my health. I'm going to say goodbye to boxing. I'm going to retire and go into the movies.

"MARVELOUS" MARVIN HAGLER,
*former middleweight champion, on
a rematch with Sugar Ray Leonard*

I'd like to get a steamroller and lay [Ken] Norton down and crush him flat. Other than that, I like him.

GEORGE FOREMAN

Looking at a fighter who can't punch is like kissing your mother-in-law.

JACK HURLEY

Hurting people is my business.

SUGAR RAY ROBINSON

Money is for spending.

SUGAR RAY ROBINSON

Boxing is the art of self-defense. You have
to pattern your style for each fight against
the style of the man you're fighting.

SUGAR RAY ROBINSON

Sugar Ray Robinson had a nice ring to it.
Sugar Walker Smith [his real name]
wouldn't have been the same.

SUGAR RAY ROBINSON

Of course (boxing) is primitive, too, as
birth, death, and erotic love might be said
to be primitive, and forces our reluctant
acknowledgment that the most profound
experiences of our lives are physical events.

JOYCE CAROL OATES

Sports in General

Whether it's politics or football, winning is like shaving: you do it every day or you wind up looking like a bum.

JACK KEMP

Sports is the toy department of human life.

HOWARD COSELL

Games are the last resort of those who do not know how to idle.

ROBERT LYND

Sports do not build character. They reveal it.

HEYWOOD HALE BROUN

Explaining something sensible to Lord Killanin [President, International Olympic Committee] is akin to explaining something to a cauliflower. The advantage of the cauliflower is that if all else fails, you can always cover it with melted cheese and eat it.

WILLIAM E. SIMON,
President, U. S. Olympic Committee

Try to hate your opponent. Even if you are playing your grandmother, try to beat her fifty to nothing. If she already has three, try to beat her fifty to three.

DANNY MCGOORTY,
billiard player

There is a function of a quasi religious nature performed by a few experts but followed in spirit by the whole university world, serving indeed as a symbol to arouse in the students and in the alumni certain congregate and hieratic emotions. I refer, of course, to football.

CHARLES HORTON COOLEY

Football today is far too much a sport for the few who can play it well; the rest of us, and too many of our children, get exercise from climbing up the seats in stadiums, or from walking across the room to turn on our television sets. And this is true for one sport after another, all across the board.

PRESIDENT JOHN F. KENNEDY

One of the greatest educational swindles ever perpetrated on American youth.

A. WHITNEY GRISWOLD,
on athletic scholarships

If I ever needed a brain transplant, I'd choose a sportswriter because I'd want a brain that had never been used.

NORM VAN BROCKLIN

You learn how to be a gracious winner and an understanding loser.

JOE NAMATH

For when the One Great Scorer comes to
write against your name,
He marks—not that you won or lost—but
how you played the game.

GRANTLAND RICE

When the one great scorer comes to write
against your name, it matters a whole hell
of a lot whether you win or lose.

A LOT OF COACHES

The key is to concentrate your way through
the bad times.

DAN FOUTS,
San Diego Chargers quarterback

Confidence is the result of hours and days
and weeks and years of constant work and
dedication.

ROGER STAUBACH,
Dallas Cowboys quarterback

Games lubricate the body and the mind.
BENJAMIN FRANKLIN

The easiest thing in sport(s) is to win when
you're good. The next easiest is to lose
when you're not any good. The hardest is to
lose when you're good. That's the test of
character.

ROY EISENHART

It is in games that many men discover their
paradise.

ROBERT LYND

Being a sports fan is a complex matter, in
part irrational . . . but not unworthy . . . a
relief from the seriousness of the real world,
with its unending pressures and often grave
obligations.

RICHARD GILMAN

Only winners are truly alive. Winning is living. Every time you win, you're reborn. When you lose, you die a little.

GEORGE ALLEN,
football coach

In the field of sports you are more-or-less accepted for what you do rather than what you are.

ALTHEA GIBSON DARBON,
Wimbledon champion

Sporting events give people time off from the problems of the world.

PETE ROZELLE,
N. F. L. commissioner

Anyone who will tear down sports will tear down America. Sports and religion have made America what it is today.

WOODY HAYES

I hate all sports as rabidly as a person who likes sports hates common sense.

H. L. MENCKEN

I always turn to the sports page first. The sports page records people's accomplishments; the front page has nothing but man's failures.

EARL WARREN,
Chief Justice, U. S. Supreme Court

I've always wanted to equalize things for us. . . . Women can be great athletes. And I think we'll find in the next decade that women athletes will finally get the attention they deserve.

BILLIE JEAN KING,
1973

Baseball

Us ball players do things backward. First we play, then we retire and go to work.

CHARLIE GEHRINGER,
Hall of Fame second baseman

I could never play in New York. The first time I ever came into a game there, I got into the bullpen car and they told me to lock the doors.

MIKE FLANAGAN,
Baltimore Orioles pitcher

The good Lord was good to me. He gave me a strong body, a good right arm, and a weak mind.

DIZZY DEAN

Don't look back. Someone might be gaining on you.

LEROY (SATCHEL) PAIGE

One night we play like King Kong, the next night like Fay Wray.

TERRY KENNEDY,
catcher

Well, this year I'm told the team did well because one pitcher had a fine curve ball. I understand that a curve ball is thrown with a deliberate attempt to deceive. Surely that is not an ability we should want to foster at Harvard.

CHARLES W. ELIOT,
Harvard President

You can't get rich sitting on the bench—but I'm giving it a try.

PHIL LINZ

A ball player's got to be kept hungry to become a big-leaguer. That's why no boy from a rich family ever made the big leagues.

JOE DiMAGGIO

Baseball is too much of a sport to be called a business, and too much of a business to be called a sport.

PHILIP K. WRIGLEY
Chicago Cubs owner

Your body is just like a bar of soap. It gradually wears down from repeated use.

DICK ALLEN

The highlight of my baseball career came in Philadelphia's Connie Mack Stadium when I saw a fan fall out of the upper deck. When he got up and walked away the crowd booed.

BOB UECKER

Why pitch nine innings when you can get just as famous pitching two?

SPARKY LYLE,
N. Y. Yankees relief pitcher

I'm no different from anybody else with two arms, two legs, and forty-two-hundred hits.

PETE ROSE

I'd go through hell in a gasoline suit to play baseball.

PETE ROSE

The Giants win the pennant! The Giants win the pennant! I don't believe it—the Giants win the pennant.

RUSS HODGES,
radio broadcaster, after the Giants'
Bobby Thomson hit the "Shot Heard Round
the World" to win the 1951 NL Playoff
with the Brooklyn Dodgers

If somebody came up and hit .450, stole 100 bases and performed a miracle in the field every day I'd still look you in the eye and say Willie [Mays] was better. He could do the five things you have to do to be a superstar: hit, hit with power, run, throw and field. And he had that other magic ingredient that turns a superstar into a super superstar. He lit up the room when he came in. He was a joy to be around.

LEO DUROCHER,
N. Y. Giants manager

The will to win is worthless if you don't get paid for it.

REGGIE JACKSON

A homer a day will boost my pay.

JOSH GIBSON,
Negro Leagues great

How can I hit and think at the same time?

YOGI BERRA

I believe that racial extractions and color hues and forms of worship become secondary to what men can do. The American public is not as concerned with a first baseman's pigmentation as it is with the power of his swing, the dexterity of his slide, and the gracefulness of his fielding or the speed of his legs.

BRANCH RICKEY,
who broke baseball's color barrier by bringing Jackie Robinson to the Dodgers

I'm not concerned with your liking or disliking me. . . . All I ask is that you respect me as a human being.

JACKIE ROBINSON

The average person can't realize what a nightmare this has been. The last 10 days of the season, all winter, spring training, right up till today. Now I'm just tired. Not let down—just tired. I'm beat.

HENRY AARON,
after hitting his 715th career home run to break Babe Ruth's record

All I can tell 'em is pick a good one and sock it. I get back to the dugout and they ask me what it was I hit and I tell 'em I don't know except it looked good.

BABE RUTH

I've never heard a crowd boo a homer, but I've heard plenty of boos after a strike-out.

BABE RUTH

It wasn't just that he hit more home runs than anybody else, he hit them better, higher, farther, with more theatrical timing and a more flamboyant flourish. Nobody could strike out like Babe Ruth. Nobody circled the bases with the same pigeon-toed, mincing majesty.

RED SMITH

I hit 'em where they ain't.

WEE WILLIE KEELER

59

I never blame myself when I'm not hitting.
I just blame the bat, and if it keeps up I
change bats. After all, if I know it isn't my
fault that I'm not hitting, how can I get
mad at myself?

YOGI BERRA

Catching is work. Hard, dirty, tough work.
Few kids want to work that hard. Most kids
have a psychological block about catching.

DOUG RADER,
California Angels manager

[The secret of my success is] clean living
and a fast outfield.

LEFTY GOMEZ

It took 15 years to get you out of a game.
Sometimes I'm out in 15 minutes.

LEFTY GOMEZ,
*to Lou Gehrig after illness forced
Gehrig out of the line-up*

When I started, it (baseball) was played by nine tough competitors on grass in graceful ball parks. By the time I was finished, there were 10 men on each side, the game was played indoors, on plastic, and I had to spend half of my time watching out for a man dressed in a chicken suit who kept trying to kiss me.

RON LUCIANO,
American League umpire

Sure, I have muffed a few in my time. But I never called one wrong in my heart.

BILL KLEM,
umpire

I always eat frog legs before I pitch. It makes my fastball jump.

RICK RICE,
Baltimore Orioles pitcher

[San Francisco's] Candlestick Park is the ninth blunder of the world.

HERB CAEN

It's drugs, the lure of easy money. Kids that would be playing in these [Little League] programs—I mean 12- and 10-year-olds—don't want to go to school or play sports. They're selling drugs. It's everywhere.

GARY SHEFFIELD,
*Milwaukee Brewers shortstop, describing
his old neighborhood in Tampa*

When you see the ball, you have a better idea where it is.

JEFF TORBORG,
White Sox manager

I became a good pitcher when I stopped trying to make them miss the ball and started trying to make them hit it.

SANDY KOUFAX

I think too much on the mound sometimes, and I get brain cramps.

BRITT BURNS,
Chicago White Sox pitcher

When you're hitting the ball, it comes at you looking like a grapefruit. When you're not, it looks like a black-eyed pea.

GEORGE SCOTT,
Boston Red Sox

A good professional athlete must have the love of a little boy. And the good players feel the kind of love for the game that they did when they were Little Leaguers.

TOM SEAVER

What do you want to throw him?

BILL DICKEY,
Yankee catcher

I don't want to throw him nothin'. Maybe he'll just get tired of waitin' and leave.

LEFTY GOMEZ,
preparing to pitch to Jimmie Foxx

Oldtimers weekends and airplane landings are alike. If you can walk away from them they're successful.

CASEY STENGEL